COPYWRITING YOUR WAY TO SUCCESS

S. Thomson

To everyone who ever knocked me down and made me stronger.

CONTENTS

CHAPTER ONE

Introduction

WHO IS THIS BOOK FOR?

Getting started with copywriting, and marketing in general, can be daunting if you've never done anything like this before.

It can seem as if there's just too much to learn and you really have no idea where to start to market your business.

This book is the first in a series of guides that aims to break down these barriers and give you ways to start building a strategy for marketing your business.

Starting with copywriting, this series will go through ways you can learn how to market your products and services to your customers.

What I hope to achieve in this first book is to make copywriting less-scary and help you realise that you really can do it yourself, but you need to be prepared to practice and to fail at times, because copywriting is a learned skill that if you practice enough, you will be able to do but you must put in the effort.

But before I get into the what's included in this guide, I need to point out that if you've picked this up thinking it was about copyrighting information in the legal sense of the word (and spelled differently) this is not the book for you.

Copywriting is part of marketing and is an integral part of any strategy to market your work. It is the words you use that sell your products or services, or to put another way, the way you express yourself as your business brand.

It is not content marketing, that will be covered in another book in the series. Copywriting and content marketing are different beasts and although, often work together, they are very different.

Copywriting is words that sell something.

Content writing is words that give free information.

Now we've covered what's not included in the book, we'll look at what is included.

The book starts by looking at the brief. This is standard in the copywriting world. In professional terms, whoever wants copywriting doing is the person who will give you the information you need to do this work; this is called a brief.

However, you might be forgiven for thinking that, as you're doing the copywriting for your own business it might be pointless to talk about a brief, but this chapter will talk you through how giving yourself a brief is a good idea to help you focus on your topic and your overall chance of success.

We'll also look at research and how researching your market and audience is important to be able to write for them. We'll examine why it's important to know what it is your audience wants and how you can write copy, that gives them what they want.

Competition is another area that is vital for copywriting and is something we don't often think of when we're a start-up, beginning our first copy project. But what your competitors are doing can really help show you how to make your copy better, by giving you info on what they're doing right, and what they're doing wrong, and how you're different. Looking at competition can help you define your USP.

We'll also look at your audience and how to focus your message towards them in their language and not get too insular talking about yourself and what you think your audience should know, which can be very different from what they actually want.

Don't believe me?

Read this chapter and see.

We'll look at headlines, how to construct good and bad ones, and how to make yours work. A headline is your first line of copy; it's your first opportunity to pique your audience's interest and get their attention and as such it's important to get right. We'll examine how you can do this.

We'll look at constructing copy itself and the general rules of writing it, and why you shouldn't let your used-car-salesmen idea of what selling is, put you off, and how copy is so much more than this.

We'll also look at how combining copywriting with content marketing can take your writing to the next level and why both are important, and how using elements of both can help interest your audience.

But not forgetting structure, we'll look at your ideal beginning, middle and ending to give you a better idea of what information should be included in each section to make your copy flow from one part to another seamlessly.

Next we'll look at style and how we all have our own style but also, how you can develop a company style, which forms part of your branding strategy.

We'll look at that most vital of things - the call to action or CTA for short - and why we need one, what the purpose of it is and why it's the most important part of your copywriting.

Finally we'll look at editing your work and problems you might encounter on your journey.

Overall this book will give you a basic level of understanding for each of the different factors that could affect the success of your copywriting strategy.

It will give you a better idea of what goes into a copywriting plan and how you can take some of these things forward in your own business.

I would suggest making notes as you go and answering any questions I pose as you move through each chapter.

Work through each section practising and developing the things I talk about for yourself. Make sure you have fun and remember copywriting is like any creative pursuit, it's not a linear thing you can formulate, you need to learn the rules and develop your brand style to attract your customers.

What works for your competitor may not work for you. It's about testing, learning, experimenting and growing.

CHAPTER TWO

Breif on the Brief

Your brief is the way you set out what you want the outcome of your copy to be. It will include things like the goals you want to achieve, the strategy of the piece, who your audience is and how you're going to reach them.

It also has things like what your offer is going to be, the tone of your copy, what emotion you'll create in your audience and the limitations.

If you make and follow your brief, your copy has a much better chance of working and doing the things you want.

WHAT'S A BRIEF FOR?

The purpose of a brief is to give yourself a set of instructions on where you are going with your writing and how you are going to get there.

Think of it like a set of blueprints to follow and on which to expand.

For a professional copywriter, a brief is standard when writing any kind of content, copy or marketing material. A freelance copywriter will be given a brief from their client, whereas an in-house copywriter will be given a brief from the project manager, or person in charge of the marketing. Sometimes, if the company is a start-up it's the CEO who gives the brief.

In your case, you are learning to write the copy yourself, so giving yourself a brief is a great way to make the whole process easier.

By planning out what your project needs, who the audience is and what the outcome needs to be, you'll then be able to work out what copy needs to be written in a much easier way than if you just guessed.

It's also a good way of getting your ideas out of your head. Sometimes by getting everything on paper, you can really examine what ideas will or won't work.

HOW TO START

So what kind of things do you need to think about?

Well that really depends on your project, but some of the more general things to start with might include:

- When you want the project completed by
- Whether you will need to interview people to complete the project
- Who you target audience is
- What you know about this audience
- What the most important problems this audience has
- Whether you need to do more market research
- How your product/service solves the problems your audience has
- What five words you would use to describe the values of your company
- Who your competitors are
- What makes you different
- How your copywriting is going to be used
- Anything else you can think of

Simply by looking at your answers and tailoring the copy to suit your target audience, you will be much closer to writing a good piece of relevant copy. I know that sounds easy for me to say, and it can be tricky at first, but it just takes a little patience, thought and practice. For example, the way you write copy to appeal to someone aged 55 would be different from how you would try to appeal to someone aged 18.

This is an obvious example that highlights the difference but, as an example of this, let's say you're selling holidays; for the person age 55 you might want to appeal to them by using words like luxury, relaxation, and gentle soft retirement style breaks, whereas for the 18 year old you'll need to appeal to their sense of fun and give them lots of excitement and entertainment.

Both audiences want a holiday, but these holidays are likely to be very different in location and activities, which affects how you write your copy.

Once you've answered the questions above, you take all this information and build a picture of who your audience is:

- What they want and what kind of things they're looking for
- What platforms you'll find them on
- What sort of advertising will get their attention
- How you can utilise this information

This all informs your choice of how you write your copy and where you write it for. The more time you spend getting this bit right, the better your chance of success.

Not all copywriting is about the copy itself, it's about how well you know your audience but more on that later.

IMPORTANT BITS

When writing your brief, what kind of things should you

consider?

Well, you start with the important things. Here's a few to get you started:

GOAL

This is simply a way to make sure you write goals that can be achieved. If you write something vague like, 'sell things', you can't really measure a goal like this. But if you say something more measurable like 'I'd like to sell 50 more boxes of my product by this date'. This is a goal you can measure. However, not all goals will be about sales, they could be more to do with branding, company awareness, positioning or even company identity. It's important to make sure you're clear about what you want to achieve, otherwise how will you know if you've achieved it? Decide now what your main goal will be.

- What is the outcome you want to achieve with this copy?
- What is the purpose of it? List these.
- Are they goals you can measure?

OFFER & PROMISE

Your offer and your promise are two different things; they work together but are different. Your offer could be a free product with a purchase of something but your promise could be a personal experience.

- What are you offering your audience?
- What promises are you making to this audience about your product or service?

BACK-UP

Make a note of the supporting evidence for the product promise/offer. Here's where you'll build your marketing argument for when you start writing. What this looks like will depend on whether your back up statement is based on appealing to their emotions, intuition or logic. This is where you prove your product/service is genuine and desirable.

- What evidence do you have to prove your product promise/offer?
- Can you use it in your copy, i.e. testimonials, reviews?
- Can you use it to argue your case?

BRANDING

Each company has their own personality - this is your brand. Your persona reflects the values your company supports and works by. It's important that each copy piece reflects the persona of who your company is.

- Is your company personality all about fun, or more serious?
- What words describe your company?
- Can you use these to reflect your company brand?

EMOTION

If you work in an industry where people are mistrustful (I'm thinking of car salesmen here) you'll need to find a way to promote trust. This also means that you have a much harder job getting people to buy, because you've got to convince them you're trustworthy first.

- What emotions need to be considered in your industry?
- Does your product/service mean you need to deal with anxiety or fear?

INFLUENCERS

Industry influencers exist in most fields. It's important to know who these people are and what they are saying about your industry. They are often ahead of the trend on things and can give useful information you may not have thought of. Don't ignore these people.

- Are there influencers in your industry you need to watch or follow?
- How can you social proof and promote yourself as an authority in your industry?
- Are there ways you can address this in your copy?

FUTURE SELF

It's important to think about how your product or service can appeal to your customers 'future self,' so they can see vision of where they see themselves, or would like to be in the future in your product or service.

- How can you use this to show that your product or service will help them get there?

TRIANGLE

This is sometimes called the golden triangle and is based on the pattern of the eye when we look at advertising copy. It is said that we first glance at the piece, then focus on the top left corner, move to the top right corner, travel diagonally to the left side and finally move down the page. This is important when considering the visual look of your copy.

- How will the copy be laid out on the page?
- Can we use bullet lists and short paragraphs and sentences to break up the text visually?

LIMITATIONS

It's important we look at what limitations we have as a company and within ourselves. These could be anything from being an unknown company so it's more difficult to get noticed, to your industry knowledge being less than you would like.

- What are your limitations?
- Is it branding, competitors, knowledge of your product or industry?
- How can you address these in your copy?

CARRY OUT

There are a number of tools to get your message out there. Templates you can use in future campaigns can be useful to save you time and get you back to running your company. There are subscription services for stock images, social media tools. Explore these and find ones that work for you.

- Are there social media tools you can utilise?
- What about email, blogging and advertising, what tools can you use for these?

CHAPTER THREE

Not Boring Research

Before you can begin to write anything decent for your website or marketing materials, you must first do your market research. I know, it's dreary and not at all why you're starting your business, but it is necessary.

DO I HAVE TO DO IT?

Market research can show you exactly who your target audience is, what's important to them and what they're actually looking for. You might think you already know this, so don't need to do this step.

After all, you know your product or service well, so surely you know your audience?

Right?

Wrong.

I can assure you with absolute certainty, if you've not done your research, you do not know your audience and probably have no idea of what they really want.

A few years ago, I left my day job as a Content and Copywriter to spend more time with my then, one year old, fourth, and final, child. So, to keep my skills up to date and not give up copywriting entirely, I decided to freelance. I assumed that as I had lots of professional writing experience I knew exactly what my audience wanted, they wanted me to write for them, they would be clambering over themselves to hire me. How wrong I was. With the words ringing in my ears of one new start up business lady,

"Why would I need you, when I can build my website and write my own content myself?"

It was then I realised, that I knew nothing about my audience, I knew nothing about what they really thought and what they really wanted. I had assumed they understood the value of professional writing, as the bigger corporations did, and where my main experience came from. Until that point I had spent my time working with companies that did understand the value of professional copywriting, but what I hadn't anticipated was that a brand-new start-up had no idea at all what the word copywriting even meant, let alone want to hire me.

I realised then, I had to go and do some real research to find out exactly what these new business start ups wanted and assumed about my industry.

This assumption nearly cost me dearly, but thankfully that lady, helped me realise that I was completely wrong.

I'm here to do this for you now. One of the biggest mistakes you can make is to assume. Think about the big assumptions you've made about your audience:

- Are there instances where these assumptions can be tested?
- Are there ways you can find out for definite?

Think about your industry:

- Is it easy for you to speak directly to your audience?
- Is there a way you can look at what your competition are doing to get a better idea?
- Could you combine a number of ways to look at

what it is your audience really wants?

Or put another way:

That assumption you've made about your customer, client or audience, what evidence do you have to prove that you are right?

Your market research is the way you prove that you are right and I am wrong, and if that's the case you have my permission to email me and tell me so.

I hope you are right but does it hurt just to check with a bit of research?

Seriously though, if you hope to write anything decent for your website, build a brand and become a professional in your field, you need to start with the research. It's the foundation of your copy strategy.

Go on, it won't kill you.

NOT SO DULL DATA

There are many different ways to carry out market research on your clients, customers or potential clients and customers. The first thing I think of is being at school handing out questionnaires to my fellow students, and them being less than compliant, but the teachers being so out of touch, they don't understand.

However, if, like me, the horror of teenage market research projects haunts you, the digital age has come about and saved us.

Hooray.

What this means for us shy people, who balk at the idea of accosting strangers, is that you can prepare and conduct your research entirely online if you wish, you can ask for respondents through social media, or through a paid service from a questionnaire company.

I'm no market research expert, as you can probably tell

from my teenage horror at the thought of it, but I do know that doing your research is important for writing content and copy. It's also vital to get insights into your category, local markets and your competition.

If you're not like me and lucky enough to be outgoing and chatty with strangers, then get yourself out and target those companies and customers. It is important that you get responses from your target audience, not just your mother.

Mother's give great answers but they won't help you in the long run.

Besides initial research, it should become a part of your business strategy, regular surveys are important to see if you're still in touch with your customers and what they want.

So, ways to conduct research could include:

- Online through a survey provider
- On paper the old fashioned way, handing them out in person
- Making phone calls to your target audience
- Finding out which social channels your customers are on
- Via social media to examine your audience's views and opinions - make a note of the words they use to describe your industry
- Keep an eye on trending content to see patterns
- Get involved with your community joining in conversations
- Ask customers who do buy how they feel about the product
- Find industry influencers and follow their social channels and blogs
- Stay away from vague questions and anything that will get a yes or no response - you want them to open up and use their own words
- Make a note of the demographics of your audience,

which is just a way of saying pay attention to their age, sex, gender etc
- Anything else that gets your potential customers to tell you what they are looking for - be creative

HOW TO USE IT

So, once you've got your research completed, how can you use that data?

Well simply, you use the data to show you how your audience thinks, what they tell you they're looking for, for example, one of the things to come out of my research when I began my business, was that not only did many start ups not know what content and copy really is but some even mistook it for the copyrighting of information, a completely different thing which is even spelt differently. This highlighted to me that not only did my target audience not think they needed my services, they didn't even know what it was I was offering or what the benefit to them would be.

This completely changed the way I was going to target this audience. Instead of just selling professional copywriting, I first had to educate with content about what copywriting is and how it can help a start-up.

If I'd just targeted that start-up audience with my assumption they would know what I do and how I can help them, all my marketing effort would have fallen flat, and potentially been very expensive mistakes. However, knowing that most start-ups had no idea what it is and why they need it, I could change the way I focused my copywriting and marketing towards that audience.

So, has your research come up with anything like this?

In my case I had to then go about trying to educate these businesses on why getting their content and copy correct is absolutely vital.

So, how do you go about doing this for your own business?

Simply through information, through the writing we're going to work on.

- With articles, videos, infographics and information about your industry and your service, that gives your customers what they want, without there being a catch
- By making yourself the expert on your industry and your subject
- Through using your audience research to get their attention
- Through using words they themselves have used.
- By answering the questions they're asking. You interact with them on the social channels they're already on being as friendly and available as possible so they see you as a trustworthy source.

A part of this will need you to do content marketing, but for the moment this book is focusing on the copywriting part of this strategy. However, both content marketing and marketing in general is needed to work together alongside your copywriting as a whole strategy.

CHAPTER FOUR

Don't Look Behind You

Whatever business niche you're in, it's pretty certain you're going to have competition of some sort. This is a good thing; it means your business product or service is popular. However, it is very important to know as much as possible about your competition and what they are doing with their online content and copy, then make yours better.

Sounds easy when you put it like that doesn't it?

WHO ARE THEY?

When looking at the competition, it is first important to find out who they are to examine what other companies are offering. It might be a good idea to make a list or spreadsheet of your findings. During the course of your research you should be looking at answering questions like:

- Who are your competition?
- What is the copy on their websites like?
- Has it been written well, has it been edited?
- Is it consistent?
- Have they developed a brand style of writing?
- Or, is it complicated, full or confusing text and

mistakes?

Although it's important to note the website design and look of their site, I want you to focus on their copywriting on their site and on their ads and marketing material. Regardless of whether your competition has a good looking site, logo or fancy website by a top designer, if their copy is badly written, they have let themselves down and their customers and clients down too.

You don't need to follow their example, what you need to do is examine who they are, and what their text is like. Really examine it, get down into the words.

- Look at the style they've used, is it chatty or formal?
- Have they been consistent with tenses or have they chopped from I to We to You all the way through so you don't know if you're coming or going?
- Have they stuck up a big square shaped block of text or is it spaced out with lots of white spaces in between the words with sentences of different lengths?

You need to examine at least three to five competitors and do an analysis on their copy by looking at:

- Style
- Sentences
- Structure
- Formality
- Ease of reading
- Call to Action (CTA)
- What is their focus?
- What are they saying their individual selling point is?
- Why would someone go to them?
- Imagine yourself as a customer, why would you choose this company?
- Why would you not choose this company?

Have they focused on their customer or have they written

their copy from an internal point of view? In other words look at whether they talk at their customers all about themselves or whether they focus on that customer.

Finding out what the value and offer your competitors are providing, is absolutely vital, and is just as important as finding out what your customers want. It's also important to note what emotional value these competitors are offering. Its more than just price and service, you need to see what their market position is.

Use your spreadsheet or chart to make a table of things like their:

- Social followers
- Tagline or slogan
- Promise
- Position in the market
- Product comparisons
- Customer testimonials or ratings
- Strengths and weaknesses
- Customer service
- Pricing
- How they're getting their message to their customers

Do this for your own company as well so you can clearly see the differences between yourself and your competitors. This will really help you see where you're ahead and where you're behind.

Then you can use the areas of strength in your own company and focus on them, while working to bring your weaknesses to a stronger position.

WHAT'S DIFFERENT ABOUT YOU?

Now you need to look at your own business.

What is it that makes you different?

This is important because, using this feature to focus your

content and copywriting strategy is what will ensure you stand out from these other businesses in your niche.

Standing out by focusing on the positive, unique aspects of your business will help clients and customers see the benefit of using your products or services over your competition.

So take a good look at yourself, your service, and products. Is there something you're offering that they aren't?

- You could be the only one who offers something a little extra
- You could be the only one who packages your products in a particular way
- You could have a unique business approach
- You could have a particular way of dealing with your customers and clients

The list is endless.

The only thing I can say with certainty is that your business is unique because it has you, now all you have to do is identify what that actually means for your clients and customers. What is it you're going to do, or can do, that's not like anyone else?

MAKE UNIQUE WORK

When you've identified what it is that makes you unique, you can then look at how to use this in your business. So if there's something your competition isn't offering that you can, make a feature of it, make this feature unique to your company. If you have a particular set of skills that your competition doesn't, make a feature of it.

You can use it in your writing by identifying the positives, by drawing their attention to this unique aspect.

So, for example:

- You might be the only one in your industry to focus on sustainability

- You could have a unique set of skills that would appeal to your audience
- You might package your product in an entirely unique and desirable way

There are lots of ways that make your business stand out and your copy will benefit if you use this in your writing. Essentially, you need to focus on the message you are trying to portray:

- What is good about your unique ability?
- Why should people care?
- Why should they be bothered by what you're offering?

Answer these questions as you write, focusing on the positives:

- How you're going to solve their problem
- How you make it easy, exciting, interesting, etc
- Highlight the benefit of using your product or service over the competition
- And most importantly, always focus on the customer and their needs

Don't spend your time talking about yourself and your company, instead talk about the benefits to the customer of using you or buying from you, for example:

- It will solve this problem because…
- It will help with…

Answer these kinds of issues to help focus your subject and make yourself different to your competition.

CHAPTER FIVE

It's Not About You

This is one of my biggest bugbears with businesses. But the simple and hard truth is that, it really isn't about you, it's not about you at all. However, many start-ups, and worse some established companies, make the grave mistake of looking from the inside out and providing copy they think their customers should know, when actually what they should be doing is focusing on what their customers actually want.

BUT IT'S MY COMPANY

Yes, Yes I know, it's your company.

But that still doesn't mean it's all about you.

Instead, what it's actually is about is your customers and clients.

To write copy successfully, you really need to get out of your own head, and into the mind of your customers.

As a practical example of this, first imagine yourself as a customer, would you find a paragraph of text like this engaging?

"We are opening new premises soon and we hope we can count on lots of people visiting us on our open day, where we will be

talking about our business and what our products are to our customers and clients."

Really?

Yawn, yawn. This is very boring, and so self focused.

Would you go to the open day?

I wouldn't.

What the company should be doing is talking directly to their customers and clients with something more on these lines:

"Open day on the 15th. Discover how Humphrey's Gold Leaf Cream will change your life, plus all visitors get entered to our prize draw to win a year's supply. So what have you got to lose? See you at 10.00am."

This isn't perfect but a lot better than the first example.

The point I'm making is that by changing your focus from yourself projecting outwards to your clients, offering them an incentive and focusing on what they want will make a huge difference to your impact and engagement.

Talk to them about the benefits of your product or service to their business or personal life.

What is the problem they have that you are solving?

Talk about these and how what you've got to offer will help.

GETTING FOCUSED

The most important word in marketing is 'you'.

This little word is going to help you talk to your clients on their level.

So instead of saying something that has lots of I words, you'll focus on the 'you' word and tell them how you're going to solve their problems.

So, what is it they need or want?

Let's say they want something free.

Two companies approach this in different ways.

One puts out the following message:

"We're giving away a free sample of our luxury cream at our open day on Tuesday."

But the second company puts out the following message:

"Get a free luxury cream when you come to Tuesday's open day."

In this instance, the change is small, but it has a big impact on the message being portrayed. The second company's message is better. That's because we as consumers are innately selfish. We don't want to hear about other people and their businesses, we want to know what those businesses can do for us, what they can do to improve and add to our own lives. The first company talks about themselves whereas the second focuses on the benefit.

So long as you remember that people are interested in themselves, and write according to this, you will be able to write copy that appeals.

YOUR TARGET AUDIENCE

Often you'll have to write something for a niche audience.

The important thing to remember is the same as above, you need to focus on what this audience wants and write accordingly.

Actually, writing for a niche target audience is much easier than writing big generalised content aimed at no one in particular.

What you need to do first is follow the steps we've set out in earlier chapters of this book. You need to identify your audience through market research and examine what the competition are doing before making sure you offer something different and unique.

Once you've done this you focus on them and what their

needs are.

- What is it about this specific audience that makes them want to buy something?
- What is the problem they need solving?
- What is the equipment they need or would like to help them?
- What would encourage them to buy from you?

This is different for every customer base and every business. The way you approach this is unique to you but it is important to get your copy correct.

Essentially you focus on niche target audiences in the same way you would for a wider audience; you find out what it is makes this audience tick, what do they need and want, and you write about your product in a way that solves this problem.

Say you're someone who sells luxury hairdryers, you wouldn't simply talk about what the speed and heat settings were. This is way too boring.

What you do is talk about how much more wonderful their hair will be using your luxury hairdryer than the cheaper one your competitors are selling.

However, I should stress here this isn't a licence to write something that isn't true, and equally it isn't a way for you to say negative things about your competitors either. Focus on the positives, highlight the benefit to your product and why it will improve their lives.

Often companies develop personas at this stage, so to make it easier to target your copy and marketing messages; you write a persona for your target audience.

A buyer must like and feel confidence in the product or service you're selling before they'll buy from you.

They must believe you know what you're talking about and you're able to give them what they want and need. This is where research comes in. Your message needs to speak to their practical side and emotional side. To do this you use your research to create typical customer profiles, often called an ideal customer persona.

This is where you develop a characterisation of the ideal person you want to buy from you. You must be able to create curiosity so they feel they need to find out more.

- What words could you use to develop an emotional response?
- Are they male, female, or other?
- Are they married, single, working, retired or at school?
- What do they do, how do they get money?
- Are they affluent?
- Do they have children?
- What are their hobbies?

You can go on getting as detailed as possible, give your customer persona a name. Consult this list every time you write so you can appeal to them.

Think about the kind of message this person responds to.

CHAPTER SIX

Topping The Headline

Your headline is your first chance to get your reader interested in your product. It is important and should be crafted carefully. Don't make the mistake of thinking that because it's short and only consists of a few words that you can shove up any old headline or title. This is a bad idea.

In the early days of the internet (and still sometime now) it became common practice among some unscrupulous people to put up enticing headlines to get people to click (click bait) and when you read the copy it had nothing to do with the title.

Don't do this.

Always make your title relevant to the copy you're writing.

BAD HEADLINES

A bad headline is easy to write, it simply takes no thought, no planning and at worst has no relevance to the text below it.

Bad headlines come in many forms, but usually they are the kind of thing that doesn't entice someone to read the words below it.

They can also focus purely on stating simply what it is, for example an article on business accounting is simply called *"Business Accounts."*

I mean, really? Would you read it?

I know I wouldn't.

Yawn.

However, if it said something like *"How to Make your Business Accounts Sparkle,"* although I hate anything to do with finance, I might read this.

It's important to make sure you're headlines sparkle.

GOOD HEADLINES

So what is it that makes a good headline?

Well a good headline entices the reader to begin reading the article. It promotes that tiny seed of curiosity, that instinct to find out more, that little voice that tells you that you simply must find out what it says.

Its purpose is to get the first sentence read. It needs to be attention grabbing and short. It's your first chance to attract customers and needs to show the emotional position of your product (in other words, it needs to appeal to them on an emotional level).

Good headlines come in many forms and the truly great ones draw you in without you even knowing you've been taken in. They can be anything including:

- Asking an enticing question
- Making a bold statement
- Promising to solve a problem
- An unusual fact
- The list is endless

Put simply, a good headline is interesting and doesn't make people turn off, click away or yawn. Instead it creates a sense of interest, mystery, excitement and even mysticism.

But however you choose to write your headline, you must

make sure it fits the subject you're writing about. Your headline must provide a way to solve the problem your readers have, if it promises something, you must deliver that promise in the copy.

You cannot promise something and then not deliver this is a complete no-no and will put you on a fast track to haters.

Take some time to scour the internet to examine headlines looking at things like:

- Do they link to the text?
- Is it good?
- How?
- Did it make you want to read more?
- How have they crafted that headline to entice you to read, or not read?

MAKE IT WORK FOR YOU

I would suggest taking your time over this bit, allowing yourself time to come up with something. Jot down a few ideas, change the wording around, does it sound better in a different way? Do you need to keep thinking?

The only thing I find with writing is that the more you put pressure on yourself to deliver, the more you find it hard to actually deliver and things like headlines can be something that no matter what you do, just doesn't go right, then all of a sudden, inspiration provides the ideal headline, usually when you're doing something else. So, what I'm trying to say is that it's really important not to stress about headlines.

With that said, I would maybe try brainstorming ideas for your headline.

The first step in this process is to write down what it is your article or content page is about, what are you talking about, what message are you delivering.

Next you need to look at what style your article is written

in, what I mean here is, what type of article or content page is it; is it a how to; is it a FAQ page; is it an article about a person; is it about something in the news, etc.

So look at what format your page is and then construct a headline to go along with this, for example, copy that focuses on how your readers can do or achieve something would naturally work well with a 'How To' headline.

I often find that headlines work best if they are constructed at the end of the writing process rather than the beginning. That way I can make sure they actually go along with my copy and coming up with something good is much easier.

However, if you prefer to do the headline first, this is fine too. It's really about what works best for you.

Some people like to come up with a working title first and then develop a better headline at the end.

Your individual style and the way you like to work and construct will dictate how you do this step.

It doesn't really matter when you come up with your headline, just as long as it's relevant, interesting, and unique.

However, if the copy you're writing is for an advert, it may not need a headline in the same way you would put one in for an article. Ultimately with headlines, always makes sure it is:

- Relevant to your copy
- Is used if needed
- Entices readers to look at your copy
- Is not spammy click bait style

CHAPTER SEVEN

The Copywriting Trenches

Copywriting refers to words written that are primarily meant to sell something to someone.

This type of writing is often where new business owners shy away. The mistakenly believe that selling is some seedy underhand tactic people use to make you buy things you don't want.

And even the term selling has become synonymous with underhand practices.

However, copywriting is so much more than this and has the potential to be so much more helpful and useful than most people realise.

If you don't learn to write copy, you really are doing your business a disservice.

WHAT IS COPY ANYWAY?

Copy is the term used in business to describe writing that is aimed at selling something. It's the main text section that tells the story of your brand. One of the defining features of copy is that it always has a call to action, or CTA for short. This is the most dominant part of your copy and is different from your offer, which is the product or promotion you're giving.

Copywriting can be to anything from advertising leaflets, text for promos, or anything at all with the intention of giving someone the opportunity to do something at the end. Even the product description on your favourite shampoo is a form of copywriting, the script for the perfume adverts that come out thick and fast at Christmas time are a form of copywriting.

Copywriting is everywhere if we take the time to notice it.

However, it is a particularly skilled art that many writers spend a lot of years developing and refining. It isn't an easy skill, but with a little practice you should be able to try a little yourself.

WHAT'S IMPORTANT

The most important thing in copywriting is getting people to read what you've written.

Now this doesn't just mean the whole piece of writing, what I actually mean is every individual line.

So, the main reason for having a headline is to encourage people to read the first line of your article.

The main reason for your first line is the get your second line read.

And on it goes right to the bottom of your article where, you will have your call to action or CTA.

The call to action is simply the action at the end you are asking the reader to take. This might be to buy something, sign up for your email list or attend an event. Whatever it is you want them to do, that is what you are selling.

The term selling, doesn't have to mean literally selling products. It might be more important for you to develop contacts on an email list at this point; it might be more important that they attend your event.

So first of all, it's important to establish what action you want your reader to take when they've read your copy:

- Do you want them to buy something?
- Visit somewhere?
- Sign up to something?
- Or something else?

Whatever it is, focusing on this is the first step to writing copy.

Think about what you're promoting - what's the best way to showcase it? Each product or offer is unique and needs to be presented in its own individual way. Your copy revolves a lot around the mental process of buying and there's so much thought that goes into writing before the act of writing begins.

HOW TO MAKE IT WORK?

So you've established what it is you are selling and why, and you know your copy needs to encourage readers to read each line.

But how do you actually do it?

Well, first and foremost, in copy, your headline is your most important line. If you don't have a good headline that encourages people to read the rest of your text, it won't matter how well your copy is written, if no one likes or clicks your headline, you're losing before you've started.

So, spend time writing a good headline that will interest your reader, that they will find useful, exciting and interesting.

If no one finds your title interesting and it doesn't make them want to find out more, they won't click your link and they won't read the amazing copy you've crafted.

First of all you need to think about what your headline must do. It needs to give the reader something, some reason, some benefit, to reading. There has to be a reward for their time.

Once you've done this, you just need to work on this strategy one sentence at a time, making sure each one makes your reader want to read the next. Start at the beginning. If they don't read your first sentence they probably won't read any more. Make this first sentence short, and intriguing so they can start to read without realising. Use a larger typeface at the top to separate and encourage reading.

Another way to make your copywriting compelling is to keep the language simple. My mother, who is an English Teacher by profession, once told me, long before I wrote for a living -

"those people who know the big words also know the little words, so when writing always use the little words."

This is so true in copywriting. Keep the language simple and compelling. However, this does not mean you have to write as if people are stupid, quite the contrary, but there's no place for long academic elaborate words of which no one knows the meaning. You're not showing your knowledge of the dictionary, even if you do know the meaning of the most complicated word in the English language.

So when crafting your copywriting the first thing to focus on, once you've got your headline sorted, is the reader themselves - make sure you've given them the offer of something in return for reading, information they want, curiosity, etc.

Next, you need to make sure each section has a reason that links to your main offer. It's important to keep tight within this and don't allow yourself to go off on a tangent.

It's also a good idea to use things like testimonials from happy customers who have had success with what you are offering, and provide data on the information you are giving.

Then it's often a good idea to talk about the reader again,

what is the reason they should pay attention, why should they continue to read?

Finally conclude by going back to what you originally promised and show how you have just given them this.

Then, and only then, can you actually make the offer. Don't shy away from this and be flimsy in your offer. Don't say things like *"if you would like…" "here's where you can find out more…"*

Instead you need to be clear and firm *"find out more today" "improve your life, get this product today"*, etc.

It's important to mention here that you shouldn't be worried about your first draft. All first drafts are terrible, unless you're some writing God who gets inspiration from a golden arc of inspiration that shines down on you as the angels sing…

Yeah right!

The rest of us mortals have to work at it. The real skill in copywriting is taking that first draft and making it shine. Adding sentences, deleting some others, it's all part of the creative process. Your goal for the first draft is to get something on the page, to make a start because you could have the best product, but if you can't communicate this, you won't have a business.

Here's some important 'don't forgets' when working on your copy:

1. If you're writing an advert, it's much harder if readers aren't genuinely interested in your product - this is where your ideal customer persona comes in
2. It's important your copy really grabs them from the beginning
3. There's no reference to benefits, features or product descriptions in the first three-four sentences, these are just to get and keep attention.
4. Create the best buying environment through your

word choice, phrasing and honesty - look back at your research into the words your customers are using themselves

5. Always aim to stop readers saying, *'I don't want it'*, *'I don't need it'* or *'it's not relevant to me'*. Address these problems in your copy to ensure you don't lose them.

CHAPTER EIGHT

Content & Copy: Combine Like A Pro

Now we've gone through the copywriting section. You might be forgiven for thinking that that's it now, there's nothing else needed.

Well this isn't strictly true because whether you're writing content or copy, you need to use elements of both to succeed.

Let me explain what I mean…

WHAT IS IT ANYWAY?

Combining content writing and copywriting depends on what you are doing.

But first it's important to look again what the differences are between the two.

Content writing is creating valuable content online for free that attracts readers, who turn into customers over time because they trust you. This type of writing is done on things like blogs, podcasts, email newsletters, vlogs, etc. It can consist of things like white papers, webinars, news bullets, industry trends, updates and summaries, media releases, blogs, or articles in magazines

Copywriting is created specifically to get your reader to

take an action. That could be anything from signing up to your email list, to buying your product. This type of writing is done on product sales pages, adverts, and mailers.

So combining is the purpose of using content writing within your copy and using copywriting within your content.

So, if you're writing a sales page, you would add in information that the customer would find useful and interesting to read.

And, if you're writing content, you add in some aspects of copywriting, like the call to action.

Successful content draws people to your company brand and creates your company as an authority on a particular subject; it builds trust in you and your brand and can help achieve visibility.

You might hear the word content marketing thrown around and this is just referring to the process that enhances your visibility so, using social media, search engine optimisation (SEO) and pay per click (PPC) are all ways you can get your content marketing message out there.

The biggest difference between content writing and copywriting is that content writing follows a more journalistic editorial style of writing whereas copywriting is written to sell.

WHY IS IT IMPORTANT?

Combining content and copywriting is a really important aspect of your online marketing strategy. And, if you can do it well, is a great way to ensure your words are read, shared and liked.

Because if you can get more people interested in your content and copy through combining the two aspects of them, your authority will increase, you will become more well known and your site will rank better because it is popular.

Combining the two aspects can be tricky if you're new to writing but it can be done with a little bit of practice.

HOW TO DO IT

If we start with content writing, we can move on to copywriting in a moment.

Some people put content online and get very little readership, then sit and struggle wondering what they are doing wrong, when in actual fact what they are doing wrong is the copywriting aspect of their content. Their articles might be great, useful pieces, but their copywriting isn't all that brilliant.

So, to perfect your content by adding in some elements of copywriting, you need to do the following:

1. Make sure headlines are engaging and not boring to read - it should state the news and tease the content to come
2. Also make sure the headlines don't have some obscure title that people don't understand
3. Your opening should be a statement of what the story is about but leaves them wanting more
4. Make sure your content shows clearly what the benefit is to your reader for sticking with it
5. Include some facts, statistics and third party endorsements if you can
6. Make sure what you write focuses on building trust and authority on your subject
7. Make sure you are doing everything you can to social proof your writing
8. And finally have a call to action at the end of your content telling them what to do next

Copywriting however, aims specifically to sell something. But it's not a magic wand and won't give you instant success.

But if you keep in mind the best practices for content writing and incorporate these into your copy, you should be able to improve what you write.

So, to perfect your copywriting by adding in some elements of content writing you need to do the following:

1. Make sure the free content you're offering is really, really useful, relevant and valuable to your reader.
2. Make sure your advert is written around valuable content, that way it is less likely to be ignored and thrown away
3. Always write for your reader. Don't get hung up on SEO and attracting search engines. Write for your customers
4. Great copy that's written with a content aspect to it, will be interesting and won't feel like used car salesman sleaze
5. Don't use those underhand click-bait tactics we talked about earlier to get attention, you're just going to annoy people, and it will not give your brand a very trustworthy reputation.
6. Make it curious but relevant to your content.
7. Always rewrite
8. Always get it proof read
9. And remember it usually takes someone five interactions with a brand before they'll consider buying from them

CHAPTER NINE

The Building Structure

Structure is sometimes one of the areas new writers struggle when it comes to copy.

However, if you learn a few simple ways to structure your copy you will find it is much easier to craft.

And, don't forget to practice, practice, practice.

START AT THE BEGINNING

The aim of the beginning is only to get your reader to keep reading.

So the purpose of your beginning sentence, should be to entice your reader to want to know what happens next.

In that sense you're intriguing their curiosity, you're getting them to want to know more.

So how do you do this?

Well, your beginning sentence should follow on from the amazing headline you wrote earlier; it should expand and explain what the headline meant, and promise what is to come if they keep reading.

Things to remember about the beginning:

- The purpose is to get them to read the first sentence

- These first sentences must be so short the reader reads before they know they've started, so things like, 'it's easy', 'you're here', etc
- Grab them so they want to find out the answer, or the info you're offering.
- Don't list benefits, product descriptions or that kind of thing here; first is to get them to read, benefits come later
- Remember it's all about their emotion; what emotions are you appealing to
- How long it needs to be depends on what you're offering. If it's something expensive, the rule is that it usually needs longer copy

MIDDLE OF THE ROAD

The middle is where you go into more details, you might focus on a benefit to them, to highlight their need for your product or service, you might use a testimonial from other users, you might use both. It really depends on the requirement of the copy you're writing.

Whatever you decide, it's important you structure it in a way that utilises the power of story, rather than just listing the features.

If, for example, you're a drinks company and your new drink is infused with berries and jujube, it'll be much more effective to tell a story of how that tastes than to just list that they are included.

This is why when we watch adverts for new products, they show people enjoying and loving that product, they don't just list the features of the product.

Think like this, tell your reader how it will make their life better and what they can get out of your product.

Feed their selfishness.

Things to remember about middles:
1. Focus on the drama, tell them something interesting
2. Make sure you're still focusing on the emotional selling point of what you're offering
3. Use persuasive writing but not used-car-salesman sleaze
4. Make your messages different - don't sound the same as everyone else
5. Avoid cliché sales power words like; incredible, guaranteed, amazing, unlimited, proven, immediately, exclusive, etc
6. Use clear simple language - stay away from long complicated jargon
7. Include evidence, figures, testimonials, stats and anything else you have to back up what you're saying, but it should be obvious that you only include things that are actually true
8. Use your research to include any words your audience already uses themselves, and that reflects their interests, personality and lifestyle.
9. Only write to your ideal reader, you can't be all things to all people, focus on the ideal persona

ENDINGS

Your end is also very important. You can craft a great piece of copy but get the end wrong and you might as well give up.

The end tells the reader what to do next, what action they need to take to move forward.

Essentially, copy is written to sell, so this is where you tell them to buy, sign up, or get in touch.

Do this well and make it as easy as possible. Don't be wishy-washy with your CTA (call to action).

Be direct, tell them what to do, make it urgent, link it to an offer, make it time limited. Help them to make the decision right now, not later.

Remove as many barriers as possible,

These could include things like:

- I'll do it later,
- I don't need this,
- I have other things to get first,
- I can't afford it,
- What's the point of this?
- Answer their questions:
- Make it urgent, make it a limited offer so they don't move on and forget about your product
- Tell them how it can improve their lives for the better
- Show them how it's helped others by highlighting how others are using the product
- Give them payment options, or levels of commitment
- Show them exactly what it is, what it does and why it is of benefit to them

Finally your CTA is really important to get that sale. Without it people will move on. Don't assume people will read your copy then buy, you need to tell them to do it.

We are all inherently lazy and have so many other distractions that, without a good CTA, people will move on to the next distraction. Tell them what to do, tell them to buy now.

CHAPTER TEN

Do It In Syle

Alongside trying to develop a personal copywriting style, you should be developing a house style, while also ensuring you pay attention to the conventions of writing copy that works.

Style is essentially copy that creates trust, authority and gets people to buy.

In this section we're going to explore this.

WHY IS IT IMPORTANT?

So why is it important to have a style, or even to follow the style conventions of copywriting.

Well there are a number of answers to this question:

1. You will have your own style of writing naturally, everyone does - it's part of who we are, like a personality trait. You may not know you have it yet, but it's definitely there and the more you write the more you learn to know what your style is.

    This is what makes you unique and it should be encouraged, rather than fought against.

2. However, there are a number of copywriting style

conventions that you need to adhere to.

Why?

Simply because they work.

They have been developed over generations, and have come about by learning the simple nature of human behaviour and what we do and do not respond to as men and women. This does not mean you can't have your own style or put your own flair on it, quite the opposite, but you need to be aware of the rules and what works before you try and experiment with alternatives.

3. A brand style is something you should be developing from the very beginning of your business starting point and not just in your writing, but your graphics, logo, presentation and how you are as people. Your brand should reflect what and who your company is and its personality - i.e. the personality you have given to it.

    Use this in your writing, use this to inform your work. Build a style sheet of words that reflect your company, then use these in your writing communication where needed.

THE CORPORATE WALL

So as a copywriter, one of my biggest problems is coming up against the dreaded corporate wall. That faceless company that hides its people, personality and drive behind virtual wall.

Don't be that company.

What I mean by this is the kind of companies whose copy is so very full of things like the following:

- Jargon no one outside of your niche has any idea about

- Very long 'business' words that are, not only, unnecessary but make you look like you're trying too hard
- Very long words in general. You're not writing an academic paper. Dump the long words
- Dull, dreary, unplanned words that are just there to fill a page
- Words that talk all about the company and how good they are, but nothing about their customer's desires
- Copy that has nothing to do with anything their customers might want, but instead reflects what the owners want

Don't be this type of company.

Keep your copy conversational, friendly, useful and focused on the customer. Tell them what they will get out of it.

You must be real.

Make your words reflect the company brand, but make that brand something customers can have trust in.

This will only happen if they get to know and learn all about who and what you are.

Keeping everything as simple as possible is the best thing you can do. A conversational, friendly style is always more preferable to dry corporate words. This is something you'll find many business can't get right. The mistake many companies make is they believe sounding professional means boring corporate language.

It really doesn't.

Professional has many forms and your writing can be professional without being dull.

You can even break some grammar rules if you want when writing copy to keep things related. Just don't tell my English teacher mother!

You'll also find style can be reflected through bullet points and numbered lists, and always focusing on your reader by using 'you' rather than 'we/I'. This will really help your style develop and keep it relaxed and visually pleasing too.

It's a common known fact in marketing that we trust messages with our names on them or that refer to ourselves more than those without.

Another way to keep your style unique is to make use of story. Everyone loves story. Just look at the big brand Christmas adverts we anticipate each November to see the power of story giving enormous brand power to these companies.

With regards to the length of your copy, without trying to sound too vague, it should be as long as it needs to be. As a general rule longer copy outsells shorter copy, but it may be that you industry, product or service doesn't need long copy. You need to look at what you're selling and decide what the length needs to be. Experiment, try different lengths and styles and see which your audience responds to. As a rule though, if your product has more features and benefits the copy should be longer. And if it's going to be on the internet it also needs to include lots of information that persuades, as internet audiences in particular, need a lot of persuading generally.

If you're not selling a product but a service, this generally needs less detail but if you are trying to make a sale, you need to overcome all their objections. This could include things like:

- I don't want it
- I don't need it
- I don't have time/I'll do it later
- It's not relevant to me

Work to overcome these objections by:

- Showing them why it'll benefit them
- Showing them why they need it in their life

- Making the offer time limited
- Showing them how it'll improve their lives

As a general guide when trying to decide what copy length should be, here's a few points to guide you:

1. An unusual product - longer copy
2. A high price - longer copy
3. A convenience product - low price, short copy
4. A shopping product - little longer than convenience
5. A specialty product - expensive luxury, longer copy
6. Products not being searched for - very long copy is needed to convince people they need your product

THE OFFER

In copywriting, there is no point in being persuasive, friendly, focusing on benefits and what the customer wants if you don't give them something.

You need to offer them something to get them to take the action you want, whether that is signing up for your email list or buying your product or service. No matter which action you need them to take, your offer needs to be something they will want and should be tailored to your ideal audience's needs.

- You add in your offer as a benefit
- Will it improve their lives?
- Will it make things easier for them?
- Will it provide entertainment?

Whatever the offer is you need to tailor your copy to go along with this. For example, if you are offering something that is for entertainment, let's say you've written a mystery thriller (go you!) and you're offering free copies for those on your email list, your offer will need to let them know why your book is a book they have to read now.

Get past their barriers.

Give reasons why each of these barriers isn't an issue.

- Make them want it by writing an enticing blurb of the story
- Make them want more by giving them something so they want to find out what happens
- Give them a price they can't refuse
- Make the offer time-limited to ensure they can't click away

Essentially, as I said earlier, give answers to their problems before they know they've asked them.

Writing is a unique experience and each writer has their own viewpoint but creativity is vital to write good copy, it's not about following a set of rules, but there are some things you should consider:

- Don't use text speak
- Don't use fancy words
- Use the language your audience uses
- Use an outline to guide you but not to constrain you
- Reviews - give evidence that supports your claims
- Open with your customers problem
- Show them what happens if they ignore this
- Use dialogue to break it up and create interest
- Give your product or service as the solution

CHAPTER ELEVEN

The Big Bad CTA

A call to action (CTA) is a really important part of copy. Without a CTA your copy isn't doing its job.

It is essentially the very last paragraph or sentence of your copy and is the part where you tell your reader what to do next.

Whether that is buy something, read something, sign up to something or go somewhere, this is the part where you tell them to go do it.

Many people new to copy think this bit is ridiculous; that we're essentially insulting people's intelligence by adding in this bit. However, you have to look at it this way - it's a fact that we're all essentially lazy people and won't do it unless directed to do so.

If we assume they know what we're talking about, people will just click away to the next distraction.

They won't click to where you want them to.

WHY IS IT IMPORTANT?

So the call to action is important because it tells your reader what to do next. Without a call to action, you're leaving one of the most important parts of the whole copy out.

But why is it so important?

Well this goes back to human nature and the study of human psychology, of which I do not claim to be an expert, but there are a number of studies that have been carried out and one of the most tried and tested methods of copywriting is the call to action.

They've read your copy, they're now convinced about what you're saying, your CTA is the bit that tells them where to get your product or service, or whatever it is you're offering.

It is encouragement for them to do one of the following:

- Get more information
- Download something they might need/want
- Enter a prize draw
- Buy the product
- Join the course
- Get/do whatever it is you're offering

GET IT RIGHT

So a call to action is one of the first things you need to decide on - essentially you're working backwards. You decide what action you want your readers to take then you write your copy into that funnel.

A funnel is a marketing term which means your copy moves your reader towards that action, in just the same way a funnel directs liquid.

Once you have decided this you can then write your copy and craft your CTA.

However, there are few important things to remember first:

- Your CTA must be relevant,
- It must be clear,
- It must be enticing,
- It must be easy for them to follow

- You don't want a CTA that involves too many different steps for your reader to do.
- It needs to be easy and something they actually want to do or get
- It's no good writing copy for one thing and having a completely irrelevant CTA
- It's the ultimate goal of your copy
- You must remember that what you offer is valuable
- Use the right words with your graphic treatment
- Only use 100 words or less
- Use a button to make it easy for them to get it
- Don't put submit or buy as your button text
- Use a different colour, or font to make your CTA stand out

WHAT ELSE SHOULD I KNOW?

Your CTA always goes at the end.

Preferably the last line or paragraph, and you should also include a hyperlink to whatever you want them to buy, sign up for if your campaign is an online one.

The reason for this is that you've worked hard though your copy to direct them down the funnel towards this point. Your CTA is the main point of your copy, it's the final thing you're asking them to do. It's the whole reason you've written the copy in the first place.

So let's assume your copy has held their attention and they're at the point of where they are ready to take action. You need to tell them what to do next in a simple, easy, direct way that continues the enthusiasm you've built over the copy.

So a sentence like "click here for info" just won't cut it, you need to be persuasive and tell them why it's good for them to click.

So if you're trying to get people onto your email list, you

might offer them a free guide, book or white paper. Your CTA might say: *"All you need to do is tell me where to send your free stuff"* which is followed by your button text, which could say: *"Yes send me a free guide."*

When your reader clicks on the button they will then be taken to enter their email information. Obviously, this only works if your copy above is relevant to the guide and how useful it is. How it creates desire for the product.

CHAPTER TWELVE

Revisions, Revisions, Revisions

The revision part is where you edit and rewrite your work. You'll find that it might seem difficult at first, but as you practice you'll find the process gets easier and you'll learn to spot mistakes sooner.

Some have argued that this is the most important part of the whole copywriting process and some very successful writers have said they are terrible writers but are excellent editors. Whatever the case for you is, you'll need to do revisions before your work is ready.

WHY DO I HAVE TO?

One of the most important things in copywriting is editing. It's your friend, it turns your awful first draft into excellent copy.

There's this myth that writers, whatever type of writing they do, sit and wait for inspiration to strike before they produce perfectly formed words from nothing, with ease, and it's all so airy, light and easy.

That's is the biggest load of tosh I've ever heard,.

Believe me it does not happen like that no matter whether

you're a famous author or a copywriter.

The secret to good writing, and good copywriting, is editing.

Editing turns it into something legible, something great.

A first draft is almost like the brain dump, you get all your ideas out of your head onto the paper and then you examine the pieces and move them around until they fit together as they should.

I actually find this the most fun part of the whole process. It's where you get to play with the words, move them around like a jigsaw and see if they fit together any better in a different way.

Editing is also about brevity, whether you can say the same thing in fewer words without losing any of the emotion and meaning. This could mean you cut whole chunks out, it could mean you rearrange sentences, it depends on you and what your first draft looks like.

Sometimes, when I'm writing, work can go through 10-15 drafts before it's right, and I'm a professional, so don't worry if you feel like it's taking a while, good copy can take ages to get right.

WHAT'S IT FOR?

So when writing your first draft I always recommend just getting all the words out there on the page regardless of whether you know they're terrible or not, just get them out of your head.

Then set about objectively looking at what you've written. You'll immediately see bits that need changing, but other parts may be more difficult and you'll find it harder to spot what's wrong. Change the obvious things first, then re-read.

Once you've done this, set about changing the less obvious things. Sometimes there will be something you know isn't right, but frustratingly you can't work out what that something is. In this case it is often better to work out what is wrong by taking a break. By moving away from your work to take a break or do something else for a while, often when you return the break has allowed distance and a different perspective on your work, and you can then edit and make it sound better.

EDITING GOLD

Editing is more than just fixing spelling and grammar. In fact it can be a lot to do with your structure and the order of words on the page.

This can be on a macro level where you look at whether your topics are in the right order, whether they are clear and it can also be on a micro level where you look at your sentence structure and word choice.

Each of these elements is important and should be examined in the editing process. I work from largest to smallest. So first I look at the overall message:

- Is it the right message?
- Is it talking about the right topic?
- Is it focused?

I can then fix any issues related to the overall message and order of topics discussed in the piece.

Once this has been done I move on to paragraph structure and whether this paragraph structure is focused on one specific topic or whether it randomly moves off onto something else. If it does, this needs fixing.

Then I look at how each sentence has been constructed and whether moving the words into a different order will change it for the better, or even combine two sentences into one for greater clarity and brevity. Then if necessary, I'll examine word choice and whether the words used are relevant, positive and convey the message I want in the best possible way.

As you write more copy, this process becomes much more fluid and you learn to do these things interchangeably, but as a new writer it might be a good idea to look at each of them individually to begin with.

A lot of this type of editing is about experimenting. Play with the word structure to see if the pieces fit together in a better way. They might, they might not, it's about experimentation.

Important things to remember about editing your work:

- Look for words like; 'that', 'and', 'if', 'it', 'know' and remove them where possible
- Look for unnecessary phrases like; 'we should consider that' and remove them
- Look at your rhythm and remove anything monotone, or which is too much of a mouthful to say - things like rhyming words or similar sounding words too close together
- Think about flow, can you improve it if you rearrange the structure and sentences?
- Remember it might take a lot of drafts before it's ready
- Read work aloud to easily spot things that aren't working

CHAPTER THIRTEEN

Problems That Get You Down

Generally most writers run into problems. These could be related to inside or outside issues. Often they aren't due to your writing itself, it's your preoccupation with other aspects of your life drawing that's drawing your attention from the task at hand.

Having said this, sometimes your copy is just terrible, with no real reason why. What I say to this is, if your writing is rubbish, then write rubbish. You can always edit it later. You can't edit an empty page.

THE MYTH OF THE BEST WAY

Those new to writing often believe they need to find 'the best way' to do something. They often want a step-by-step guide on how to get the results they want. It's just human nature to want a guide to show the way through something difficult.

However, the trouble with this approach is that it can limit your ability to get the copy you really want.

It's this limiting belief that you need to learn the best way that's the issue. It stems from wanting to avoid mistakes, but it's these very mistakes that show you how to write copy well. It's only through practice and doing it badly you can learn to write well. Mistakes will help you more, as creativity isn't a linear thing that you can write a uniform set of instructions for. Instead you have to feel the best way through. Sometimes it'll be easy and you'll sit down and the words will almost flow from you. You'll feel like you're flying as each words comes out perfectly following the last.

This happens rarely.

Believe me it's not a daily occurrence, it's not even a monthly occurrence.

Most of the time it'll be hard, each word will be like giving birth - a damned hard slog and you'll write, rewrite and rewrite again until you're sick of the words and you're dreaming of the damned thing.

But it's during these hard times that you'll learn more about the process of writing copy than at any other time.

But the most important thing to remember:

There is no formula.

TOO MUCH, NOT ENOUGH

One issue is that some people find they write and feel like they've finished but are disappointed when there's not a lot of words on the page, despite feeling like they've covered everything.

Are you one of these people?

I am.

When this happens it usually means that even though you've covered all the points necessary, you may not have covered them enough, or to put it another way, gone into enough detail.

In this case it's probably worth going over each point and expanding on it to make it clear, but not too much so you end up with the opposite problem.

However, a lot of writers actually have the opposite problem to this and find that they over write. They add in absolutely everything possible and it makes their work waffly and boring.

The good news is for these people is it's easier to edit when you have this type of problem, it's just a case of cut, cut, cut.

Be ruthless with yourself, ask whether what you've added is going to help the reader make a positive decision, or whether it is going to have the opposite effect.

Once you think you've cut enough, cut some more because inevitably you'll still need to.

This is where further editing and restructuring on a sentence level may help you to cut your words down to a more useful length by trying different words and sentence formats to try and say the same thing in a shorter way.

COMMON STICKY POINTS

Copywriting is only useful if what you're selling is something people want. If you spend time writing the best copy in the world but no one wants your product, no amount of good copy will help you.

However, sometimes copy can be blamed for the failure of a product when actually the fault lies in the lack of research into the audience, desire for the product and the offer not being strong enough.

Take care that your problem isn't that what you're offering is just what people don't want, because if this is the case, you'll never sell anything, no matter how good your words are.

So, as a checklist then make sure your problem isn't that:
- No one wants your product
- Your offer is not strong enough
- People don't want what you're offering

- You don't know your audience enough
- You're marketing to a place where your audience isn't
- You don't really know how your audience views the world and what messages they'll respond to
- Your USP isn't clear

However, despite this, sometimes the problems are your copy itself and you need to go back and fix what's wrong.

The good news is that it's much easier to fix, rewrite, edit and chop something on a page than an empty blank space.

As a guide here's five ways to help you write copy if you're stuck. Use each step as a section and answer the question to each as part of your piece, making sure to write for your audience.

1. Begin with the end - you need to understand the reason you're writing the piece for the copy to work. What is your goal? In copywriting this is usually to persuade something. What's the idea behind this?
2. Once you know this, write questions on what things your audience doesn't understand, but needs to be clear on once they've finished reading. This step is important to successfully get to step one
3. Use a working headline that highlights the promise you're making to your readers with your copy. Why should they be interested in it?
4. Use these steps to form the basis of your work and answer each of the questions in as simple and clear way as possible
5. Edit, edit, edit.

CHAPTER FOURTEEN

Conclusion

WHAT NOW?

Marketing has changed vastly since the birth of the internet, and today those building a strategy need to focus their message on the internet more than offline methods that would have been their main strategy before the internet. Also with each year more and more businesses are writing copy, producing content and trying to attract customers to their brand online; it makes it harder for smaller start-ups to get noticed, particularly if they don't have a marketing budget.

In terms of copywriting, this means that it can be difficult to get the people who would love to buy your products and services to see your copy, let alone buy.

Some people take a very pessimistic view of this and think,

"What's the point in learning to write good copy if I won't be seen above these big budget brands. I might as well not bother learning and just write what I want."

Well there's a number of reasons why this is a bad idea.

1. You're never going to build a business with that attitude

2. There's no point competing with the big boys, it's better to find your own niche and focus on carving out an audience in that area

3. The more work you do on each of the points in this book the better your results will be at finding and attracting your audience

4. Because you're small, it actually means getting your copy right is absolutely vital. The big boys have deep pockets for advertising and can rely on people knowing their brand and trusting it. You haven't got that, so building and creating a branding message, that aligns yourself as being trustworthy and reputable, will really help drive your company forward.

Copy is a form of creativity and you should allow your creative side to lead as you develop and build your own brand style.

Once you've decided on your brand, write it down in a style sheet. Note your brand colours, fonts, writing tense, style, address and any other information that will help you in the future.

I hope that now you've been through this guide you have a much better idea of how to use copy, where it's needed and how to write it and you can move forward with a clear simple strategy that helps your business grow the way you want it to.

But don't forget, it's about sustainable consistency, time and effort. It won't happen overnight.

The next book in this series is the content writing guide and aims to show you how to use content writing alongside the copy you've learnt here.

Well I think it's about time you stopped reading and got writing.

Happy Copywriting.

About the Author

S. Thomson has been a content and copywriter for almost a decade and also writes in many other formats. During that time she's worked as both in-house copywriter in marketing departments and freelance in her own company.

She's also an author of fiction as non-fiction under S. Thomson.

She has a Bachelor of Arts degree in English Literature and a first class Masters degree in Creative Writing. Alongside this she has completed a number of other professional courses and taken part in business start-up programmes, so knows exactly how hard it is to start and build your own company.

She's currently working on more titles in both non-fiction and fiction, alongside running her marketing agency.

If you'd like to find out more visit https://sarathomsonauthor.co.uk and https://stwriter.com

Printed in Great Britain
by Amazon